MUSIC GETS THE BLUES

BY JESSE MCDERMOTT

PEARSON

Scott
Foresman

Editorial Offices: Glenview, Illinois • Parsippany, New Jersey • New York, New York
Sales Offices: Needham, Massachusetts • Duluth, Georgia • Glenview, Illinois
Coppell, Texas • Ontario, California • Mesa, Arizona

What's in a Name: The Blues

The phrase "the blues" has been a part of the English language for at least two hundred years. As early as 1800, people who felt depressed would say they were experiencing "the blues." But during the 1900s, the phrase acquired another meaning, one based on a uniquely American form of popular music.

It's no accident that the **genre** of popular music called the blues received the name that it did. The very first blues musicians were African Americans who grew up in the Deep South in the years prior to World War II. At the time, many African Americans endured formal discrimination, as well as bitter poverty. The songs that blues musicians sang reflected those harsh conditions, providing the blues with their mournful quality.

Blues music, as it has matured, has intersected with other genres, and that process has created new musical styles. This book describes how the blues has influenced popular music. Keep reading to learn more!

What Is the Blues?

The first recording of a blues song was produced in 1913, but blues historians speculate that blues music is older than that. Recording was difficult during the infancy of blues, so most music was performed live. This created a lack of early blues records, hampering blues historians' efforts to pinpoint the exact date of the genre's **inception.** But the available sources indicate that sometime during the late 1800s the first authentic blues music appeared.

Today's blues songs are usually performed by a singer or guitarist who's accompanied by a backup band. But the music from which modern blues developed was much different.

The first people to sing blues-style songs were enslaved West Africans who lived on pre-Civil War plantations in the American South. They could not afford musical instruments. From sunrise to sunset, those people toiled in the fields. To relieve boredom and pass the time, they would "call out," or sing. Sometimes the calls provided work-related instructions, but more often they were lines of a work song that someone had made up. The other workers would respond to the line by repeating it or adding a new one.

This style of music struck a chord deep within the West African spirit and continued to reverberate throughout American popular culture. Also referred to as the *call-and-response* technique, it has influenced rap lyrics, public demonstrations, and even the style of sermons favored by African American preachers. By having the audience share in the creative process, call-and-response emphasizes the shared experiences that unite both the person leading the call and the people responding. But as you will read, the call-and-response technique was only one of many influences that shaped early blues music.

The enslaved West Africans who worked on Southern plantations used music as a way of easing their suffering.

Ingredients of the Blues

The enslaved plantation workers sang not only call-and-response work songs, but also religious songs, called *spirituals*. These spirituals, which became a staple of African American church music following the abolition of slavery, asked for divine assistance from higher powers and, like the call-and-response work songs, helped enslaved West Africans to forget about the pain and drudgery that they endured in their lives.

By blending the musical styles associated with call-and-response work songs and spirituals, African American musicians developed the blues. Soon, they began playing the blues on instruments, such as banjos, guitars, and harmonicas.

So what makes a blues song? It depends on whom you ask. Some say that the blues is a way of thinking and singing about the things that happen in your life. Others think that a song is a blues song only if it follows certain musical guidelines. The question gets more complicated when we consider how much the blues has changed over the years. As the blues evolved, it **spawned** different styles, which were often named for the area where they developed.

Crossroads have special significance in blues culture. The Delta Blues originated around Clarksdale, Mississippi, where this crossroads is located.

One of the oldest forms of blues music is the Delta Blues. Its name stems from its place of origin in the cotton-growing regions of Mississippi, just upstream from where the Mississippi River forms its delta in southern Louisiana.

Many musicians are familiar with the structure of Delta Blues songs. A song's structure is like a map. Experienced musicians, with knowledge of the structure, can play a blues song as a group without practicing it.

So what does the structure of a Delta Blues song include? It often contains *blue notes*, notes not expected in a particular key. They lend an emotional

tone to a tune. The structure will also maintain a certain style of lyrics. Consider the following Delta Blues lyrics, which are among the most famous in blues history:

I went down to the crossroads, tried to flag a ride,
I went down to the crossroads, tried to flag a ride.
Nobody seemed to know me, everybody passed me by.

Do you notice that the first line is repeated? A verse in the Delta Blues style usually begins with two identical lines, which are followed by a third line that rhymes with the first two.

The King of the Delta Blues

The lyrics on the preceding page were originally sung by Robert Johnson. Johnson, acclaimed as "the King of the Delta Blues," led a life shrouded in mystery. For years, blues historians struggled to piece together the essential facts of Johnson's life, including when he was born, to whom he was related, where he lived, and when and how he died. Now, however, most blues scholars agree that Johnson was born on May 8, 1911, in Hazlehurst, Mississippi.

Johnson's family was poor, and they moved around frequently in search of work and a place to stay while Robert was young. Eventually, they settled in Robinsonville, Mississippi, which was steadily gaining a reputation as the center for the Delta Blues. While a teenager, Johnson built himself a primitive guitar and soaked up Robinsonville's blues scene. By the time he was a young man, his guitar-playing ability had surpassed that of nearly all his **mentors.**

In 1930, Johnson's wife died, leaving him childless. Facing bleak prospects as a sharecropper in Depression-era Robinsonville, Johnson took to the road as a nomadic blues musician. With each town he played, his reputation as a blues **prodigy** grew.

Between 1936 and 1937, Johnson recorded a total of twenty-nine songs. They became some of the most important blues songs in history, and his powerful musical style was widely imitated by other blues musicians. During the 1960s, Johnson's music became popular among a group of young rock-and-roll musicians. Johnson's influence on these musicians and their music created a dramatic impact in both rock and roll and other genres of popular music.

Robert Johnson is seen by many as the most important musician in blues history.

A Living Legend

B. B. King is a living legend. Like Robert Johnson, King's style of blues has influenced many other forms of popular music. Born in 1925 in Indianola, Mississippi, B. B.'s original name was Riley. King learned the blues using the guitar he bought and launched his musical career while still a teenager. In 1947, after having earned minor fame in Indianola for his street-corner blues, King migrated north to Memphis, Tennessee, in a quest to become a professional blues musician.

King earned the nickname "Blues Boy" while working at a radio station in Memphis, Tennessee. He later shortened the name to simply "B. B.," which stuck. Another legendary name, "Lucille," also became associated with King during this time. As the story goes, a fire broke out at a concert that King was giving one night in nearby Twist, Arkansas. King raced out of the building, only to risk his life by plunging back into the flames in order to rescue his guitar. After hearing that the fire had been caused by two men who had been fighting over a woman named Lucille, King, in a humorous touch, decided to christen his guitar (and all of his guitars since then) with that same name.

B. B. King with his guitar, Lucille

King's music eventually came to inspire a new generation of musicians who adopted his techniques for many different genres. His powerful singing voice influenced numerous pop singers, and many rock-and-roll guitarists borrowed from his smooth style of guitar playing. Most impressive of all was the manner in which he combined his singing and guitar playing, echoing the call-and-response style that originated among enslaved West Africans. King would sing a line and then play a response on his guitar, almost as if his voice and guitar were one instrument.

JAZZ Branford and Wynton Marsalis

BLUES

REGGAE Julian Marley

RHYTHM AND BLUES
Aretha Franklin

ROCK
Aerosmith

As the blues traveled throughout the United States, it played a role in the development of many genres. It is common for musical genres to influence each other. This chart shows how some of the genres have influenced others.

RAP
Run-D.M.C.

COUNTRY Willie Nelson

Country Music and the Blues

Country music is one of today's most popular styles of music, but did you know that the first country artists were influenced by the blues style? It's true! The following pages examine the relationship between country music and the blues.

The roots of American country music extend back to the fiddle tunes of the British Isles, which were brought by Scottish settlers in the 1700s to the mountainous regions of the southeastern United States. The tunes evolved over the years in response to the changes in American culture and life.

American country music took a major leap forward in August 1927 when Jimmie Rodgers made his first recordings. As a teenager, Rodgers worked on the railroads of the Deep South and was greatly influenced by the work songs of the African American railroad workers with whom he toiled. Later, when Rodgers became a professional musician, he toured the South and gave performances alongside blues musicians who also influenced his style.

One of Rodgers's earliest recordings, "Blue Yodel #1," displayed his affection for the blues. The song combined elements of the blues with Rodgers's own distinctive country style of singing, called **yodeling.**

Rodgers was not the only country musician who recorded blues-style country music that August. The Carter Family also recorded that month. As with Rodgers's tunes, the Carter Family's songs demonstrated an unmistakable blues influence. For example, their song, "Worried Man Blues," followed the same structure as most Delta Blues songs:

If any one asks you who composed this song,
If any one asks you who composed this song,
Tell him it was I, and I sing it all day long.

The Carter Family changed country music's focus by emphasizing their vocals. Earlier country musicians, mainly fiddle and banjo players, rarely sang, but the Carter Family sang in all of their songs, accompanied by guitars and other instruments.

With songs such as "Worried Man Blues," the Carter Family mixed aspects of the blues with traditional country music.

The Blues and Early Rock 'n' Roll

As you now know, the blues had a major influence on country music. However, its impact on rock and roll was even greater, to the extent that it is credited with having given birth to rock music.

Rock and roll was invented in the 1950s, having **coalesced** from a combination of the blues, country, and **rhythm and blues.** Many of the first rock and roll songs, such as the 1954 version of "Shake, Rattle, and Roll" by Bill Haley and His Comets, were older rhythm-and-blues tunes that had been modified.

Rhythm and blues, like rock and roll, came from the blues. It's characterized by the same blue notes and emotional quality found in the blues. Rhythm and blues and early rock and roll shared many attributes, as artists in both genres relied on blues themes, lyrics, and song structures for inspiration.

As much as the blues influenced rock music in the United States, it had an even more substantial effect on young musicians in England, whose love of the blues would change the sound of rock and roll forever. In the early 1960s, young English musicians started listening to recordings of American blues greats, such as Robert Johnson and John Lee Hooker. At first, they just mimicked the songs that they listened to.

Eventually, though, they began to incorporate the blues into their own music, which often fluctuated between rhythm and blues and rock and roll. The result was a new kind of rock music called blues rock. Blues rock kept the strong beat that rhythm and blues had brought to rock and roll, but it also used the structure of the blues, along with signature blues features such as blue notes.

In the early 1960s, the Yardbirds were among the first English rock musicians influenced by American blues musicians.

Eric Clapton: A Rockin' Bluesman

Many English musicians who came of age during the early 1960s developed into great blues rock players. Of them, Eric Clapton might be the greatest.

Clapton, born in 1945, became infatuated with the music of American blues legends, such as Muddy Waters and Robert Johnson, as a teenager. Clapton would practice Johnson's songs for hours, until he learned to play them perfectly. Soon he was able to move past simply duplicating old blues songs and on toward developing his own style.

As Clapton improved, he attracted the attention of other English musicians, who were eager to have him perform with them. During the late 1960s, Clapton earned famed as a dazzling young rock blues guitarist while playing with the Yardbirds, John Mayall's Bluesbreakers, Cream, and Derek and the Dominoes. In 1971, he launched a successful solo career.

In 2000 Eric Clapton realized a lifelong dream by recording an album with blues legend B. B. King.

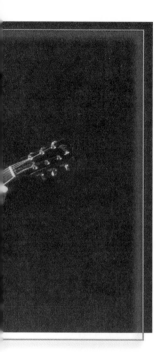

Over the past couple of years, Clapton has recorded a few tribute albums, acknowledging the blues greats who influenced him. In 2000 Clapton recorded an album with B. B. King who, along with Robert Johnson, was one of the heroes of Clapton's youth. In 2004 he recorded an album that took him back to the start of his career. Entitled *Me and Mr. Johnson,* it consisted entirely of Robert Johnson songs that Clapton had reworked.

Thanks to Clapton, a whole new generation of fans have been introduced to B. B. King, Robert Johnson, and other original blues greats. Though Clapton's experiences as a white Englishman were very different than those of his African American blues idols, his love of their music and his talent for playing the blues has bridged that cultural gap.

The Blues Worldwide

The blues, beyond having helped give birth to country, rhythm and blues, rock and roll, and blues rock, is also responsible for having influenced several other types of popular music.

Pop rock, although not as dependent on guitar playing as the blues and regular rock and roll, owes much of its emotional style of singing to B. B. King and other blues greats. Jazz music was developed in New Orleans and St. Louis during the early 1900s by African American musicians who shared many of the same experiences as Robert Johnson and other early blues artists. It has borrowed heavily from the blues.

Reggae music was influenced by the blues sound that was carried to Jamaica and other Caribbean islands by African Americans. Rap music and hip-hop have roots in a kind of blues called "talking blues," as well as reggae. Even modern classical music, which developed in an environment that was completely different from the one that nurtured the blues, has incorporated elements from blues music.

The blues has played a powerful role in the shaping of modern popular music. Its widespread influence and worldwide popularity should give it success for years to come!

The Blues and Its Descendants: A Brief Time Line

1913: The first blues song is recorded.

1927: Jimmie Rodgers (right) and the Carter Family become the first country music artists to make recordings. Their music is highly influenced by the blues.

1936–1937: Robert Johnson records twenty-seven songs. His music would have a great impact on rock and roll.

1950s–1960s: Rock and roll and rhythm and blues develop as separate genres, distinct from the blues. Musicians in both genres rely heavily on the blues for inspiration, however.

1960s: Rock and roll helps B. B. King and other bluesmen gain national exposure.

2000: Eric Clapton honors his blues roots by recording with B. B. King.

Now Try This

Your Favorite Band and the Blues

As you have read, Eric Clapton has done much to acknowledge the blues musicians who inspired him. Have you ever thought about who might have influenced the musicians you like to listen to? There is a good chance that your favorite musicians were influenced by the blues!

The following activity will give you the opportunity to find out which blues artists have influenced your favorite bands. Follow the steps on page 23 to learn about the artists that your favorite band looks to for inspiration.

B. B. King influenced Eric Clapton, who, in turn, influenced many other artists.

1. List some of your favorite bands. Choose one of them to study more closely. Go to the library or use the Internet to track down books, magazine articles, and other information about your band.

2. After you find your sources, read them over and make notes of any references they make to your band's musical influences.

3. Write the name of your band in the middle of a piece of paper. Draw a circle around the name. Then draw a line extending out from the circle. On that line, write the name of one of your band's influences. Keep doing this for all of the influences that you are able to find.

4. Look at the influences that you have listed. Were any of them blues musicians? If you don't know the answer to this, use the Internet or some other source to find out. See if you can find out what type of musicians influenced your favorite band.

Glossary

coalesced *v.* grew together; united as a whole

genre *n.* a type of artistic, musical, or literary work

inception *n.* an act or process of beginning

mentors *n.* trusted counselors or guides

prodigy *n.* a highly talented child or youth

reggae *n.* popular music combining blues and rock and roll that began in the Caribbean

rhythm and blues *n.* popular music that began in the United States, influenced by the blues

spawned *v.* brought forth; gave birth to

yodeling *n.* style of singing characterized by changes from an ordinary voice to a very high voice and back again